Contents

Words in **bold** can be found in
the glossary on page 31.

The gift of the Nile

The Ancient Egyptians lived in North Africa along the River Nile, the longest river in the world. They were ruled by powerful kings, known as pharaohs. The Egyptian **civilization** began over 5,000 years ago and lasted for more than 3,000 years.

Muddy marvel

Egypt was known as 'the Gift of the Nile'. Every year the River Nile flooded after snow melted in the mountains higher up the river. The floods left behind silt, a type of mud which made the soil good for growing crops. Most of Egypt was hot, dry desert. Nothing would grow there, so people lived in the **fertile** strip of land alongside the River Nile.

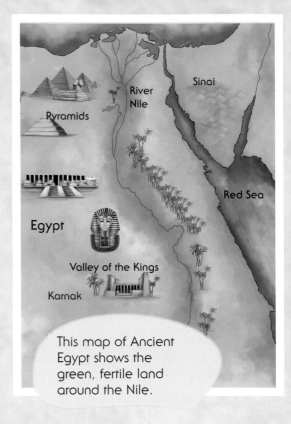

This map of Ancient Egypt shows the green, fertile land around the Nile.

This picture shows the strip of land good for farming along the banks of the River Nile, and the desert beyond.

4

River of life

As well as for watering crops, people used water from the Nile for washing and doing laundry. The Egyptians loved swimming, and the river also allowed them to travel around easily by boat. Mud from the river banks was used to make bricks to build houses. **Papyrus** reeds growing along the river bank were harvested to make fishing boats, mats, baskets, paper and sandals.

Papyrus grows along the banks of the River Nile.

Dangerous waters

The river was not always the safest place to be. The waters of the Nile were home to crocodiles and hippos, both of which were known to attack and kill people. Doing the laundry in Ancient Egypt could be a very dangerous job!

TRUE!

The Ancient Egyptians believed that if they prayed to the crocodile god, Sobek, he would keep them safe from crocodile attacks.

Nile crocodiles are believed to kill hundreds of people a year.

Farming

Most Ancient Egyptians lived off the land. They kept farm animals such as goats, pigs, chickens and geese, and grew crops like wheat, lettuces, grapes and melons in the rich Nile mud. Their year was divided into three seasons.

In autumn, after the Nile flooded, the farmers ploughed their land and sowed their seeds. They dug channels across the fields and built **shadufs** (right) to lift water from the river to **irrigate** the crops.

From March to July, farmers harvested their first crops of wheat and barley to make bread and beer. They then planted and harvested vegetables and fruit such as onions, lettuces, garlic, cucumbers, beans, dates, grapes and melons.

The floods arrived in July and during this time farmers did other work, including working on irrigation channels, mending tools and doing building work for the pharaoh.

The Nile is Egypt

Sing this song as though you were an Ancient Egyptian,
giving thanks for the gifts the River Nile gives you.

2. And after the flood we welcome the mud,
   The perfect conditions to plant and to grow.
   We labour and toil, we plough up the soil,
   We water the fields and get ready to sow.
   Soon the little green shoots will appear,
   Turning to barley and wheat,
   Fruits will follow and vegetables,
   Giving us plenty to eat!

3. The flood level drops, we harvest the crops
   Give thanks to the Gods for another good year.
   With plenty to spare, enough and to share,
   We know that for now we have nothing to fear.
   This is life on the banks of the Nile,
   This is why Egypt is strong.
   We the people are safe and secure,
   Proud to be singing our song!

Daily life

The Ancient Egyptians were skilled builders and **craftsmen**. They built many great structures, including pyramids, the Great Sphinx (right) and lots of beautiful temples. They worked hard, but they enjoyed family life and spending time with friends too.

The Great Sphinx and nearby pyramids at Giza took thousands of men many years to build.

Work

In most families, men worked as farmers, builders or craftsmen. Women looked after the household and children, made beer, spun thread and wove cloth. Wealthier men might work as **scribes** or collect **taxes**. Rich families had many servants.

This wall carving shows some Ancient Egyptians baking bread.

Food and drink

Egyptians ate one main meal a day. Most families ate a simple diet of bread, vegetables and fish, with beer to drink. Richer people enjoyed lavish banquets where they ate meat, cakes and fruit and drank lots of wine!

TRUE!

Most Egyptians had trouble with their teeth. The flour used for baking bread contained lots of sand so their teeth got worn down.

Music and games

Ancient Egyptians of all ages enjoyed singing, dancing and making music. They also enjoyed sports such as athletics, wrestling and archery. Children played with toys, including balls, toy animals and spinning tops.

An Egyptian and his wife playing a game of senet.

Senet

All Egyptians enjoyed playing the board game senet, and the famous pharaoh Tutankhamun (see pages 14 & 19) is said to have owned four beautifully decorated senet tables. Here is how to play.

You will need: two players, some card, a dice, 10 playing counters (such as tiddlywinks or buttons) in two different colours.

Make a playing board like this on a piece of card:

1	2	3	4	5	6	7	8	9	10
20	19	18	17	16	15	14	13	12	11
21	22	23	24	25	26	27	28	29	30

Rules

1. Each player needs five playing counters of the same colour.

2. The first player lays counters on squares 1, 3, 5, 7 and 9, while the second player lays them on squares 2, 4, 6, 8 and 10.

3. The aim of the game is to move all your counters around the board until they have passed square 30 and left the board.

4. Each player takes turns to throw the dice to see how many squares they can move forward. Players must then choose a counter to move that number of squares around the board. You can move any of your counters that you like BUT…

You must not land on a square that already has one of your own counters on it.

If you land on a square that already has one of your opponent's counters on, you swap places.

All counters must move around the board in a reverse 'S' shape, following the numbers in each square.

If a player throws a one, four or six, he or she gets another throw.

The first player to get all five of their counters off the board is the winner. Have fun!

9

Fashion and jewellery

The Ancient Egyptians paid great attention to their appearance, and both men and women wore jewellery and make-up.

Fine clothes

It was very hot so the Egyptians wore as little as possible, and children usually wore nothing at all. Clothes were made of linen which was woven from flax, one of the crops grown along the Nile. Men usually wore a linen kilt which was just a strip of linen wrapped round their waist and tucked in. Women wore a long, straight linen dress.

Hair and make-up

Both men and women wore make-up, in particular **kohl** eye-liner. They wore blue or green eyeshadow, while women also wore red **rouge** on their lips and cheeks. Everyone had their hair cut very short and wore wigs. On special occasions women would wear a cone of scented fat on top of their wigs. In the hot Sun, the fat would melt and trickle down the woman's wig, making it smell nice.

TRUE!

Preserved wigs have been found with headlice still in them!

This wall painting shows that both men and women wore linen.

An Ancient Egyptian wig and jewellery dating from the 13th century BCE.

Jewellery

Everybody loved to wear jewellery, such as headbands, bracelets, anklets, rings and decorated collars. Poor people would wear simple jewellery, while richer people's jewellery might be decorated with **semi-precious** stones.

Make an Egyptian collar

Decorated collars like this one were very fashionable in Ancient Egypt. Why not try making one yourself?

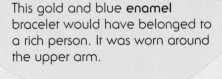

This gold and blue **enamel** bracelet would have belonged to a rich person. It was worn around the upper arm.

1. Draw a circle with a 7cm radius on a piece of card.

2. Draw a circle with a 15cm radius around the first circle.

32cm (approx)

3. Cut out the centre and a section of the collar to make it fit properly around your neck, as shown above.

4. Colour or paint your collar and decorate it.

5. Punch 4 holes, one in each of the corners at the back of the collar.

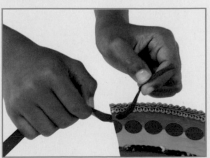

6. Cut 4 lengths of ribbon or cord and tie one into each hole.

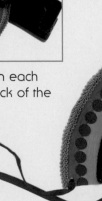

7. Your collar is now ready to wear!

The pharaoh

The pharaoh was the most powerful person in Ancient Egypt. As well as being king, he made the laws, ruled the army and was the chief **priest**.

The **burial mask** of the famous Pharaoh Tutankhamun.

A living god

The pharaoh was believed to be the son of the Sun god Ra, and was thought to be half-man, half-god. As chief priest, the pharaoh carried out the most important religious **rituals** and ordered that many fine temples be built to honour the gods.

At war

The pharaoh would go with his army into battle. Over the years, the ancient Egyptians fought many wars against neighbouring countries to protect themselves from attack, or to **conquer** new lands. If they won the war, the conquered peoples had to accept the pharaoh as their new ruler and offer him their finest treasures.

The pharaoh rode a horse-drawn chariot into battle and carried a bow and arrow.

TRUE!

The name pharaoh comes from a word meaning 'great house'.

12

Make a pharaoh's crown

This is the Blue Crown, the Khepresh, which pharaohs wore at special **ceremonies** and in battle. It was made of cloth or leather and decorated with gold discs. Here is how to make a Khepresh of your own.

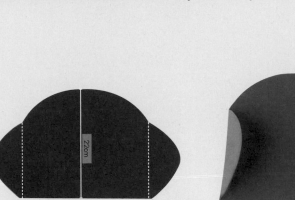

25cm 22cm

1. Copy this shape onto some blue card and cut it out.

2. Fold the side pieces forwards and make a 4cm cut up from the bottom of each fold line.

3. Cut a strip of gold card 60cm long and 5cm wide. Slot it into the two cuts on the crown and glue it into place.

4. Cut out the Uraeus (cobra snake shape) from gold paper.

5. Glue the tail onto the centre of the crown above the headband.

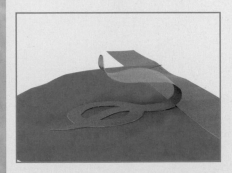

6. Using a pencil, curl the front of the snake up into an 'S' shape. Draw on two little black eyes.

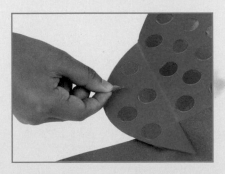

7. Stick or paint gold spots onto your crown. Fasten the ends of the headband together to fit your crown around your head. Your Khepresh is ready!

13

One kingdom

The first pharaoh is believed to be Narmer (sometimes known as Menes). At that time, Egypt was divided into two different kingdoms, Upper and Lower Egypt. Narmer brought them together into one kingdom under his rule in around 3100 BCE. After Narmer, hundreds of pharaohs took the throne of Ancient Egypt. Most, but not all of them were men.

A carving that shows Pharaoh Narmer punishing an enemy.

TRUE!

Pharaoh Hatshepsut was the first female pharaoh, but statues often show her as a man (below).

Famous pharaohs

Hatshepsut (1479-1458 BCE) Famous queen who sent traders and explorers to East Africa.

Tutankhamun (1343-1325 BCE) Known as the boy king. Became pharaoh at the age of nine and died suddenly aged about 18. He was probably the most famous pharaoh of all because of his treasure-filled **tomb** which was discovered in the Valley of the Kings in 1922 (see page 19).

Ramses II (1303-1213 BCE) Ramses the Great was the second longest ruling pharaoh. He built many famous temples and monuments, such as the temples at Abu Simel by the shores of Lake Nasser.

Cleopatra VII (51-30 BCE) Famously beautiful queen who tried to stop the Romans taking over Egypt. She killed herself when she failed, and Egypt became part of the Roman Empire, so Cleopatra was the last pharaoh.

Walk like a Pharaoh

Sing a song for the pharaoh! Use this picture of an Egyptian procession to make up your own mime or dance to go with the song.

♩ = 66 *With a lumbering gait (in 2)*

1. Walk like a Phar - aoh in a sol - emn pro - ce - ssion,
2. Freeze for the Phar - aoh as we stand to at - ten - tion!
4. March with the Phar - aoh to the King's cor - o - na - tion,

Bow down be - fore him as he pass - es by!
Just like a pain - ting on a tem - ple wall.
Dance to the mu - sic as he leads the way,

Praise him and gro - vel, make a good im - pre - ssion,
Still as a sta - tue, that is our in - ten - tion,
Wave and be hap - py! It's a ce - le - bra - tion,

'Cos

1. Last Time V.4 End here

Phar - aoh is the King! He is the King! He's a liv - ing God! God! He's a liv - ing God!

2. *f* God!

3. He is so ve - ry pow - er - ful, mag - ni - fi - cent and mast - er - ful,

He holds the keys of life and death in his hand, He is so grand and glor - i - ous,

p

al - might - ty and vic - tor - i - ous, And when he

Back to the sign

speaks, ev - ery wish is our comm - and!

Gods and goddesses

The Ancient Egyptians worshipped hundreds of different gods and goddesses. They built beautiful temples to honour them.

The Egyptians believed that their gods and goddesses gave people help and protection and should be kept happy with offerings. One of the most important gods was Ra, the Sun god. He was believed to sail across the sky every day in a boat and disappear every night, just like the Sun itself.

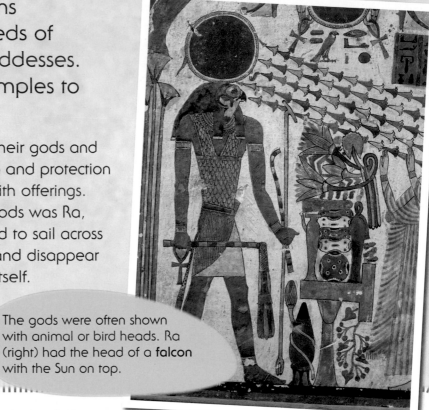

The gods were often shown with animal or bird heads. Ra (right) had the head of a **falcon** with the Sun on top.

Great gods and goddesses

Name	Role	Appearance
Amun	King of the gods	Ram's head
Ra	Sun god	Head of falcon with the Sun on top
Hapi	God of the River Nile	Headdress of water plants
Anubis	God of death	**Jackal's** head
Horus	God of the sky	Falcon's head
Hathor	Goddess of love and joy	Headdress of cow's horns with a Sun between them
Thoth	God of wisdom	Ibis (bird) head
Bastet	Goddess of the home	Cat's head

Thoth

Anubis

Places of worship

The Ancient Egyptians worshipped their gods in huge temples. The pharaoh often ordered a temple to be built to honour one particular god. The temples were made of stone and beautifully decorated.

Temple life

Hundreds of priests and priestesses lived in the temples. They carried out rituals, such as making offerings to the gods. At the centre of the temple was the **sanctuary**. This was a small room containing a statue of the temple god. It could only be entered by the high priests and the pharaoh. The temple also included schools, food stores, workshops and libraries.

TRUE!

The pharaoh and high priests had to wash before entering the temple sanctuary.

The ruins of many temples, such as this one at Karnak, can still be seen and visited in Egypt today.

Pyramids and tombs

The Ancient Egyptians believed that after they died, they made a journey to another world where they would begin a new life. They wanted to keep their bodies and belongings safe for their new life.

Burial

Ordinary Egyptians were buried in the sand in the desert. This helped to preserve their bodies for the **afterlife**. Rich people paid large sums of money to be buried in underground rooms called tombs, along with things they believed they needed in the afterlife, such as jewellery, weapons and even games and food.

Pyramids

The richest Egyptians of all, the pharaohs, were sometimes buried in splendid structures called pyramids. They could take up to twenty years to build and involved thousands of workers. The tomb itself was hidden deep in the heart of the pyramid, where the pharaoh and their rich treasures were believed to be safe from robbers and animals.

TRUE!

Rich people would have little model figures of servants, called shabtis, buried in their tombs with them to look after them in the afterlife.

The pyramids of Giza were built between 2560 and 2540 BCE.

Valley of the Kings

From about 1500 BCE, pharaohs were buried in tombs carved out of the rock in the Valley of the Kings. This was found at the edge of the desert on the west bank of the River Nile. The pharaohs hoped their tombs would be hidden in the rock and remote enough to be safe from thieves but the only tomb that wasn't robbed was that of Pharaoh Tutankhamun. His tomb was hidden under another, bigger tomb.

The temple of Hatshepsut in the Valley of the Kings.

A gold mirror case from the tomb of Tutankhamun.

Tutankhamun

The discovery of his tomb with its famous golden treasures has made Tutankhamun the most famous pharaoh of all. He became pharaoh when he was nine but Egypt was really ruled by his uncle Ay, the Grand **Vizier**, and Horamheb, leader of the army. Tutankhamun's sudden death at the age of 18 led to accusations of murder particularly as Ay became the next pharaoh, but it is more likely that Tutankhamun died in a hunting accident.

Mummies

The richest and most important Ancient Egyptians, including the pharaohs, were **mummified** after their death. This made sure that their body was preserved for the afterlife.

Dead bodies **rotted** quickly in Egypt, so mummification had to happen soon after someone had died. This was known as **embalming**. It followed strict rules.

TRUE!

Not just people were mummified. Cat, dog and even crocodile mummies have been found!

1. The internal **organs** were removed with hooks and wires and put into **canopic jars** (right) to be buried with the body.

6. Finally, the body was placed inside up to three decorated, body-shaped coffins (centre), one inside another. It was now ready to be buried.

2. The body was put in a bath of salt which removed all the moisture and left the skin like leather. This took 40 days.

5. The body was then covered in a linen **shroud** and tied up with more strips before being **blessed** by the priest.

3. Next, the body was rubbed with oils and stuffed with sawdust and linen pads to make it look lifelike again.

4. Gold coverings were put over the fingers and toes before they were wrapped in linen strips. **Amulets** (right) were hidden in the strips as they were wrapped.

The Mummy Song

The Pharaoh Tutankhamun died unexpectedly when he was just 18 and his funeral and mummification had to be done very quickly. Sing this song to send Tutankhamun on his final journey.

This model of Tutankhamun was found in his tomb.

The final journey

After it had been embalmed, a mummy was carried by boat across the River Nile to its tomb. Relatives of the dead person, priests and sometimes even musicians and dancers would follow the mummy to its final resting place.

An Ancient Egyptian funeral procession carries a mummy on a boat towards the Nile.

The Opening of the Mouth

Before it was laid to rest, a **ceremony** called the Opening of the Mouth was performed so that the mummy could breathe again. The coffin was then sealed in a stone sarcophagus and placed inside a decorated **shrine**. All of the person's belongings were piled into the tomb before it was sealed with a special label, called a cartouche, with the person's name written on it in **hieroglyphs** (see opposite).

The god Anubis is shown here carrying out the Opening of the Mouth ceremony on a mummy.

Make a hieroglyph cartouche

The Ancient Egyptians wrote in hieroglyphs, which were a cross between letters and pictures. **Historians** couldn't understand what hieroglyphs meant until the discovery of the Rosetta Stone (left) in 1799. This had the same piece of writing on it in three languages: hieroglyphs, Demotic (an Egyptian type of writing) and Greek. By comparing the three scripts, historians were able to work out the meaning of the hieroglyphs.

Use the picture on the right to copy the outline of a cartouche on to a piece of card. It should be around 30 cm tall and 15 cm wide. Cut it out with some scissors.

Write your name on the cartouche using the correct hieroglyphs from the alphabet below.

Decorate your cartouche with some Egyptian pictures and symbols. Remember that the Egyptians loved bright colours and jewels!

How do we know?

In order to understand ancient history, historians need to collect pieces of **evidence**. They put the pieces together to make a picture, just like a jigsaw puzzle.

Finding out

Historians learn about Ancient Egypt in a variety of ways. **Archaeologists** dig up and study objects such as broken bits of pottery or the remains of buildings. Historians study paintings, writings and wall carvings, all of which can tell stories about things that happened in the past. Today, modern techniques such as **CAT scanning** and X-ray are also used to give more information about the objects that archaeologists find.

Wall paintings help historians learn about ways of life in Ancient Egypt.

Archaeologist Howard Carter examines the sarcophagus of Pharaoh Tutankhamun.

Tutankhamun's tomb

One of the greatest sources of evidence about the Ancient Egyptians was the discovery of the unopened tomb of the pharaoh Tutankhamun in 1922 by archaeologist Howard Carter (see left). When Carter opened the tomb, it was packed with golden treasures, furniture and other objects, as well as the coffin of the young ruler.

TRUE!

X-rays revealed that Tutankhamun had suffered a broken leg and a blow to the back of his head.

History Detective

Historians and archaeologists work just like detectives to find out all about the past. Would you like to be a history detective?

1. 3. If you want to solve the mys - ter - y,
2. If you find a piece of pot - ter - y,
That
A

makes up anc - ient His - tor - y,
bit of arch - ae - ol - o - gy,
And if you re - ally want to be ef - fec - tive,
Con - si - der eve - ry - thing and be se - lec - tive,

You must gath - er up the ev - i - dence, Then work out how it all makes sense,
Is it fake or is it rea - lly old, 'Cos all that gli - tters is not gold!
Then
'Cos

work out how it all makes sense,
all that gli - tters is not gold!
And then you'll be, yes you'll be a His - tor - y De -
And then you'll be, yes you'll be a His - tor - y De -

tec - tive!
tec - tive!
His - tor - ry De - tec - tive!

New dis - cov - er - ies!
Look - ing at a clue,
Lost for cen - tur - ies!
Is it rea - lly true?
Read - ing all the wri - tings
Build - ing up a pic - ture

on the wall,
of the ways
Search - ing out the de - tails great and small.
Peop - le used to live in old - en days.

25

Wonderful Things

Tutankhamun is known as the boy king because he became pharaoh of Egypt when he was just nine years old. During his short rule, Tutankhamun made important changes, including moving the capital of Egypt back to Thebes and re-building many ruined temples. Tutankhamun died aged just 18 and the cause of his death remains a mystery.

Cast

- **Tutankhamun** aged nine
- **Umi** his friend, also aged nine
- **Lord Ay** Tutankhamun's uncle, Grand Vizier, acting ruler of Egypt
- **Horamheb** General and head of the army, acting ruler of Egypt
- **Howard Carter** Archaeologist
- **Lord Carnarvon** Carter's employer
- **Evelyn** Lord Carnarvon's daughter
- Newspaper reporter
- Two Egyptian workers, Egyptian citizens, courtiers etc.

Props

You will need the following items:

- *A senet board and counters (see p.9)*
- *A pharaoh's crown (see p.13)*
- *A pharaoh's jewelled collar and bracelets (see p.11)*
- *A special ceremonial robe or cloak*
- *A drum and beater*
- *A newspaper reporter's notebook and pencil*
- *A stick about one metre long to act as a testing rod*
- *A candle*

Any other props, scenery or costumes that can be provided will make your play look even more special, but are not absolutely necessary.

SONG: "The Nile is Egypt"

Scene 1 *(Tutankhamun and Umi are sitting on the floor playing senet. Umi jumps to his feet and punches the air.)*

Umi: That's it! I win! I win!

Tutankhamun: Lucky! Just 'cos the gods are smiling on you. I'll beat you next time. Best of three!

(Umi starts to object, then remembers who he is talking to and sits down.)

Umi: Yes, Sire!

Tutankhamun: Oh don't be an idiot, Umi! You're my friend.

Umi: But you're the pharaoh. I'm supposed to let you win!

Tutankhamun: What would be the fun in that?

Umi: That's what your Uncle Ay told me. That I must respect you and obey you and do whatever you want.

Tutankhamun: Just because he's the Grand Vizier and has to run the country till I'm an adult. But just you wait and see. One day when I'm grown up, I'll show him!

Umi: Ssh, Sire! He's coming!

Tutankhamun: I don't care! I mean it. *(Enter Lord Ay. He looks cold and angry. With him is General Horamheb, who is rather fat. They are followed by a crowd of courtiers, priests and Egyptian citizens, all part of the coronation procession.)*

Lord Ay: Good morning! Good morning! And how are we today?

Tutankhamun: *(a bit cheeky)* I'm very well, Uncle. How are you?

(Ay ignores this and stares meaningfully at Umi who gets the message, jumps to his feet and scuttles out.)

Tutankhamun: Why did you do that? We were just about to play another game.

Lord Ay: It's time, Your Majesty. Time for your coronation.

Tutankhamun: *(Sighing)* Do I have to?

Horamheb: Your Majesty, you are the pharaoh. The most powerful man in the world. You must be crowned. The people expect it.

Tutankhamun: But I'm not a man. I'm still just a kid! And if I'm so powerful, why can't I do what I want?

Lord Ay: Don't worry, Your Majesty. General Horamheb and I will take care of everything until you are old enough to rule on your own. And we all have to do things we don't want to do. It's called duty!

Tutankhamun: Well it all seems pretty boring so far. Lessons! Ceremonies! Duty! It's hot today. I don't want to stand for hours with all those people watching me. In fact I don't really want to be pharaoh at all!

Horamheb: (Shocked) Your Majesty! Don't speak like that. The gods will be angry and will punish us all!

Tutankhamun: (Getting up reluctantly.) I know, I didn't really mean it, but it was better before my father died, when I could just be an ordinary boy and play with my friends.

Lord Ay: You can still see your friends when your duties permit. I will arrange for the boy Umi to visit you again next week.

(Tutankhamun rolls his eyes as courtiers come forward to dress him in his ceremonial robe, collar and crown.)

Lord Ay: (Whispering aside to Horamheb) We're going to have to keep a close eye on the little brat!

SONG: **"Walk like a Pharaoh"** (During the song there is a grand procession involving everybody, escorting Tutankhamun to his coronation. For tips on this see the song on page 15)

SCENE 2: (As the song ends, a slow, continuous drum beat begins and people come running in, fearing bad news.)

Citizens: (All talking at once) What's the matter? What's happened? Sounds like the funeral drum! Has somebody died?

(Everybody is confused and upset. Enter Lord Ay followed by General Horamheb, both looking very serious. The drum beat stops.)

Lord Ay: My people! I bring bad news, the worst. Our pharaoh, His Majesty Tutankhamun, is dead.

28

(Shock, horror, gasps all round.)

Citizen: But how? He's only 18. How did it happen?

Horamheb: The gods have taken him from us.

Citizen: Why? Was he injured? Was he ill?

Citizen: Was he attacked?

Lord Ay: *(Angrily)* How dare you suggest that he wasn't properly protected! It was a hunting accident. The most important thing now is to arrange for his body to be embalmed without delay. General Horamheb and I will organise it at once.

(Exit Lord Ay and Horamheb quickly, leaving everybody else gossiping, confused, upset and a bit suspicious.)

SONG: **"The Mummy Song"**

SCENE 3

Reporter: It is 26 November 1922 and we are in Egypt, in the Valley of the Kings, on the edge of the desert, a few miles from the River Nile. It is hot and dusty and in a gloomy passageway beneath my feet, the British archaeologist, Howard Carter, together with his patron, Lord Carnarvon, and his Lordship's daughter Evelyn, are about to open a tomb which is 3,000 years old!

(As the reporter speaks, we see Carter, Lord Carnarvon and Evelyn followed by two Egyptian workers moving cautiously towards the sealed door of the tomb.)

Carter: Here we are. The final barrier. Behind this door I believe we shall find the burial chamber of the boy pharaoh, Tutankhamun.

Lord C: Provided it hasn't been broken into by tomb robbers like all the others.

Carter: True, but somehow I feel this one is different. Worker, hand me the testing rod if you please. I shall first make a very small opening just up here on the left and insert the rod to see if the way beyond is open.

(Carter makes a small hole in the barrier and inserts the rod cautiously. It goes all the way in.)

Carter: Nothing! *(He starts to widen the hole)*

Evelyn: Be careful, Mr Carter! The air inside may be poisoned after so many centuries.

Lord C: Very sensible, my dear. A candle for Mr Carter!

(The second worker passes a candle to Carter which he holds up to the gap to see if it stays alight.)

Carter: The flame is still alight. The air is clear.

(Carter widens the hole a little more and peers inside. There is a pause as his eyes adjust to the darkness and then he gasps.)

Evelyn: What is it?

Lord C: Can you see anything?

Carter: *(Turning around, looking amazed.)* Yes. Wonderful things!

(Lord Carnarvon and Evelyn crowd round and they all peer through the hole.)

Lord C: It is full of treasures. Statues, caskets, alabaster jars!

Evelyn: And a throne, and chariots. And gold! Gold everywhere!

Carter: And look! All of them marked with the cartouche of Tutankhamun. This is it! An unopened pharaoh's burial chamber. The tomb of the Pharaoh Tutankhamun!

Reporter: It would take Howard Carter over ten years to empty the chamber. He knew that every single item needed to be labelled and catalogued so that nothing would be lost of this, the most important historical discovery ever made.

SONG: **"History Detective"**

Glossary

afterlife - a new life that begins after death

amulet - a lucky charm

archaeologist - someone who digs up objects to find out about the past

bless - to make something holy

burial mask - a mask placed on the face of a dead person during a funeral

canopic jars - jars used by the Ancient Egyptians to store a dead person's organs

CAT scanning - a way of looking inside a body using computers

ceremony - a special occasion, such as a wedding or a funeral

civilization - a group of people with their own organisation and culture

conquer - to defeat (in battle)

craftsmen - people who make objects

embalm - to preserve a body

enamel - a hard, shiny coating

evidence - proof of something

falcon - a fierce bird of prey

fertile - able to produce healthy crops

hieroglyphs - a cross between letters and pictures

historian - someone who studies the past

internal organs - parts located inside the human body, such as the stomach and lungs

irrigate - to bring water to a place

jackal - a type of wild dog

kohl - a black powder used as make-up

mummify - to stop a body from rotting by embalming it

papyrus - a plant used to make mats, boats and other things, including a type of paper

preserve - to keep something from rotting

priest - a holy person

rituals - a series of actions performed in a set way, often as part of a ceremony

rot - to go bad

rouge - a red or pink powder used as make-up

sanctuary - the most holy part of a religious building

sarcophagus - a stone coffin

scribes - people paid to write for other people

semi-precious - pretty, but not very valuable stones, such as turquoise

shaduf - a machine used to move water from one place to another

shrine - a holy place

shroud - large pieces of cloth that were used to wrap a mummy

taxes - money paid to the government

tomb - an underground room where someone is buried

vizier - an important official who helped the pharaoh to run the kingdom

worship - to give thanks and pray to a god

31

Index

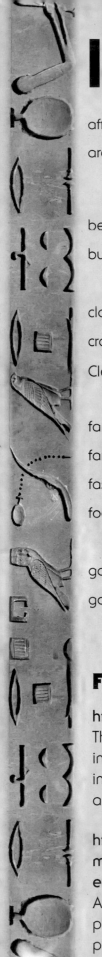

Find out more

http://www.ancientegypt.co.uk
The British Museum has lots of information on life in Ancient Egypt, including everyday life, gods, pharaohs and mummies.

http://www.childrensuniversity.
manchester.ac.uk/interactives/history/
egypt
A fun interactive site with timelines, puzzles and wordsearches, as well as plenty of information.

Note to parents and teachers: every effort has been made by the Publishers to ensure that these websites are suitable for children, that they are of the highest educational value, and that they contain no inappropriate or offensive material. However, because of the nature of the Internet, it is impossible to guarantee that the contents of these sites will not be altered. We strongly advise that Internet access is supervised by a responsible adult.